WHY YOU SHOULD NOT BE A DOCTOR

THE HIDDEN SIDE OF MEDICINE

PATRICK EDWARD NASSIR, DO

Editor: Edward Levy

Cover Design: Matt Davis

CONTENTS

THE HIDDEN SIDE OF MEDICINE

I want people to understand what medicine is *really* like today. When people hear the word "doctor," they envision a life of glamour, money, and power. Shows like *ER* and *Grey's Anatomy* focus on the dramatic, sexy aspects of medicine and ignore the complicated bureaucratic reality. In my experience, true day-to-day practice is overrated. There are many "hidden" non-clinical duties that physicians face daily. Physicians are subject to regulations, lawsuits, excessive documentation, and are often controlled by non-clinical personnel in the for-profit healthcare system. They also spend many years and hundreds of thousands of dollars in training and are at higher risk for suicide. While the actual clinical practice of medicine is great, everything else surrounding it is not.

AN ATTENDING'S NOTE

When I was in medical school and residency, most of our focus was on learning medicine. As it should be. But I wish someone had told me at least something about the state of medicine today. Burnout, while now a bigger part of the national discussion, was rarely talked about. Resident physicians who had mental breakdowns from the stress of work were sent on "leave," and the problems causing them to break down in the first place were ignored. As an attending, the money increased significantly but so did the problems. No one ever spoke to me about private equity, insurance companies, or hospital systems' profit. In some cases, profit takes precedence over everything. I feel at times as if my sense of autonomy has been stolen from me; I work not for the patient but to make others rich *at the expense of the patient*.

No one forced me into medicine. It was my choice, but I did everything they told me to. I went through college, medical school, and residency. I passed my board certification. I put my time in, time I will never get back. But this isn't what I was promised. Instead, I work for a bloated, money-driven system that gets worse every day.

I hope to shed light on the aspects of physician practice not talked about, and how the pursuit of money perverts the best of intentions. I want those planning to enter the medical field to know what they might be getting into, and those in residency to be aware of what may lie ahead. Being a physician does not mean you have money, power, or status. It means you are placed front-and-center in a corrupt system that exists to steal from the vulnerable and take advantage of the naïve. With COVID-19, these issues were exacerbated immensely. The pandemic has shown just how many cracks there are in the healthcare system—and every day it gets worse.

NON-CLINICAL DUTIES

Take it from about half of all attending physicians: They hate their jobs.

A survey conducted by Medscape in 2019 shows that about 44% of physicians are suffering from being "burned out" [1]. Being burned out, as defined by numerous large medical associations, is lacking empathy for patients, being emotionally exhausted, and feeling decreased satisfaction from your achievements. Essentially, you feel no passion for your work and every day is a drag.

But why? You should be happy as a physician, right? You'll have money, probably a nice car and house, and a comfortable life. You're telling me that 44% of people in the medical field who make hundreds of thousands of dollars a year are not happy?! How can that be? Can the job really be that bad? They must just be big complainers.

Well, yes, it can be that bad. There are a multitude of reasons why a physician might feel burned out. You might wonder why the practice of clinical medicine takes up so little of your day; physicians face an ever-increasing amount of non-clinical tasks to deal with. Or, you might be frustrated with the system as a whole.

You might make more errors, and you might do drugs and alcohol, and patients may be less satisfied with you. You'll also be at higher risk for suicide [2].

These are not just fairy tales. And while those in the medical field might tell you it's a "you" problem, this could not be further from the truth. As you will see, the blame lies with the entire healthcare system you have to work under and with.

TOO MUCH DOCUMENTATION AND THE ELECTRONIC MEDICAL RECORD

If you don't practice medicine yourself, you might wonder why you spend so much time waiting when you visit a physician. The reason is partly documentation and charting. Usually, physicians are bogged down by navigating the electronic medical records (EMR) system. Imagine if a physician went into a patient's room, interviewed and examined the patient, placed some orders, and then simply went into the next patient's room. You might say to yourself, isn't this the way things are meant to work? Isn't that what a physician does? You might be surprised to know it is typically not the case.

Physicians spend loads of time documenting. They have to review the chart (medications, past medical history, etc.), and make changes as necessary. They document a history of the illness and their physical exam. They must record a thorough assessment and plan. Usually, they also need to include special statements to satisfy government quality measures (called the Merit Based Incentive Payment System, which is discussed later). These can include speaking to the patient about their blood pressure or telling the patient to stop smoking. They can choose not to include this though they may be penalized. They also document their interpretation of laboratory results, imaging tests (like x-rays or CT scans), and other tests; they describe what their plan is with these results. They write orders, prescriptions, and consult specialists. They document discussions with specialists. They record changes in the patient's status, re-evaluations of the patient, discharge summaries, and medication reconciliation notes.

The documentation does not stop there. To bill for their services, physicians include "codes" in their charts. These codes are often confusing and convoluted, and their criteria are changed frequently. There are different types of codes physicians utilize, but for the sake of simplicity, "Current Procedural Terminology codes" (or CPT® codes) will be the focus here. Which CPT® code is used depends on how complicated it is to manage the patient. For example, a physician documenting on a simple patient might use the code "99201." If the patient is more tricky to manage, a different code is used. This other code requires additional documentation on the patient's chart. Confusion arises when trying to understand which code goes with each patient. To make matters worse, CPT® codes must be linked to other types of codes, adding more complexity.[1] If a physician does not include everything a code requires, they will be paid less, or even denied reimbursement. Residency and training typically do not prepare physicians adequately on how to use these codes. Most new physicians are left to learn this elaborate coding system on their own. They may lose money and their sanity in the process.

This is quite a number of things to record. It can be exhausting. With certain electronic medical records, this can take a while. Why not see the patient and do the chart later? While this might seem like a good idea, who can remember

40 or more individual patients? And who wants to spend hours completing charts at home?[2]

Taking a look back at the survey, we see what the first item contributing to burnout is. Paperwork! Charting! The amount of charting physicians do is crazy! And if a physician wants to write less—well, she can't! She won't get paid!! And God forbid if that same physician has a lawsuit—the prosecutor would eat her alive! And to think physicians have to do this for *every* patient encounter, especially if they see many patients a day. You can see why they might get a little tired of it.

Now, don't get me wrong. The need for documentation is understandable. Billing and continuity of patient care—these things make sense. But is there not a better way? Do physicians really need to have four years of medical school and three to seven years of residency just to spend most of their time charting? No. It's horrible, and some health-care systems agree it's horrible. At conferences where physicians come together, they all agree that it is horrible. Yet it remains.

Documentation is annoying enough, but the EMR makes it even worse. That wonderful, fantastic EMR. You must use it every day, whether you are an emergency room physician or a dermatologist.

Patient encounter? Every one must be recorded in the EMR.

Order? Each one must be placed (eventually) in the EMR.

Prescription? You better believe you need to record this in the EMR.

You saw the patient across the room and locked eyes? Must be recorded in two EMRs (a joke, but it often seems that way).

Let us do an experiment right now. If I were to walk into

my workplace and ask all my colleagues how they feel about the EMR, what do you think they would say?

"I love it."

"It makes me feel whole."

"I enjoy long walks on the beach, margaritas, and perusing the EMR."

No! Absolutely not! It is a disaster to use. No matter how many companies or people seem to work on the EMR, one thing remains the same: It is a slow, unwieldy, molasses-based piece of equipment created to increase the amount of clicking, typing, re-typing, and overall daily frustration. It's slow. It crashes. It doesn't include what you want. You can't figure out how to order something. It deleted all your work. How do you get to the previous records again? Can't I just write things down? Why is this taking so much of my time?!

To make matters worse, imagine the scenario of physicians working in multiple hospitals. Every hospital might have a different EMR! So physicians have to learn how to work a system that feels like pulling teeth, and then they have to learn it at multiple places.

The EMR also allows for tracking of physicians. How long did it take the physician to see the patient? To order? To put in their re-evaluation note? To discharge the patient? The tracking of medical staff is something administration adores, and physicians will likely be even more tracked in the future.

Some readers might point out that scribes exist to help with this issue. A scribe is an assistant who types up the history, exam, and some of the chart. While this might work to alleviate some of the headache of charting, it has a number of limitations. The scribe needs to be trained and has to understand your personal style of charting. If you work at an organization with a lot of scribes, then be prepared to be reviewing your charts quite a bit. If you can find a scribe who consistently works with you and knows how to chart the way you like it, then great! But in my experience, you still need to spend time reviewing and editing your charts. Nobody wants to do that.

ADMINISTRATION AND ADMINISTRATIVE DUTIES

For physicians who choose to go into either a group, clinic, or hospital practice where administration is omnipresent, be prepared to have a host of extra non-clinical duties. Administration is a big, big fan of numbers and statistics. As such, from time to time, you may be spoken to when one of those numbers is lacking or low.

Consider a physician who practices in the emergency room. He or she is tracked for:

- How many patients they see an hour
- How fast it takes them to say hello to a patient
- How fast it takes them to order a test on a patient
- How fast it takes them to re-evaluate a patient
- The time it takes to discharge a patient
- The time it takes to admit a patient
- The time until they consult a specialist
- The number of consults on the case
- The number of critical patients they see
- The amount of procedures they do
- The amount of prescriptions they write
- The percentage of narcotic prescriptions written
- How much money their charts are making
- How fast it takes them to complete their charts
- How many tests (CT scans, etc.) they do in comparison with their colleagues
- Whether or not they handled certain critical cases

(such as strokes, heart attacks, etc.) within the allotted time
- How much money they are making for themselves, the hospital, and the company
- Patient-satisfaction
- Where they are physically in the hospital—patient room, desk area, etc. (In some emergency departments (EDs), physicians must wear GPS trackers.)
- And more . . .

These are only *some* of the items a physician might be tracked for. Crazy, isn't it? You may not personally have to deal with administration, but more and more physicians are being tracked and judged with metrics and are altering their practice because of it. You can make an argument for needing to track physicians, as some physicians might take their time or might not be practicing in an efficient style. But at what point does it become too much? If a patient needs a CT scan and your department states, based on tracking, that you are doing too many CT scans, is it in the patient's best interest not to do one? Should you prioritize time metrics over what a patient needs clinically?[3]

Certain companies require electronic learning to be completed online for corporate compliance. They might, for example, ask you to obtain a certificate for treating some medical condition, such as strokes, even though you completed a residency in that area. Did you follow the correct protocols? Did you document everything you did? The paperwork seems endless.

GOVERNMENT REGULATIONS

If you work as a physician in the United States, you will become familiar with the Merit Based Incentive Payment System (MIPS). This system was created by Congress to increase the quality of healthcare. It judges physicians on things like the overall quality of their care, how they improve their care, cost, and if they promote the electronic exchange of health information [3]. The better they do, the higher the points they receive. At the end of the year, the government will then compensate or penalize providers based on how many points accumulated. It can be thought of as trying to get high score in a really complicated, boring, and ultimately pointless video game. If you win, you might get a small pat on the back. If you lose, you lose big.

Although Congress created the system to increase health-care quality, the system adds more to physicians' collective hassles. A physician trying to comply with MIPS has to submit insane amounts of information to the government. This data is very detailed and complex. For example, to comply with the MIPS quality measure, a physician must provide:

- Electronic Clinical Quality Measures (eCQMs)
- MIPS Clinical Quality Measures (CQMs)
- Qualified Clinical Data Registry (QCDR) Measures
- Medicare Part B claims measures
- CMS Web Interface measures
- The Consumer Assessment of Healthcare Providers and Systems (CAHPS) for MIPS survey [4]

These items are very complicated by themselves. For instance, to comply with the MIPS clinical quality measures physicians can't prescribe certain medications for certain diagnoses. They can't order certain imaging tests for certain clinical scenarios; MIPS will penalize them. Physicians must, must, *must* tell the government that they really did talk about high blood pressure with the patient. It is like having an intense helicopter parent questioning every medical decision you make. "Naughty doctor!" they might say if you mess up. "You know that's not allowed!"

The list for these regulations is huge, and physicians are expected to know and comply with all of them. And this is only one measure described; there are still many other parts of MIPS. Physicians can't ignore MIPS either. Those who do suffer a whopping 9% penalty to their compensation [5].

Not only are physicians required to know what these measures are, they have to submit data from over 70% of their patients. They must do this every year. This complicated labyrinth of a system causes smaller practices to struggle, as they spend time and resources trying to understand MIPS. These practices often need extra staff to help with MIPS, as it changes frequently. Larger corporations are able to better game the system and "win." The system is not fair to individual practices.

MIPS is another unnecessary non-clinical burden physicians deal with. MIPS adds time, unnecessary hassle, and is overly complex. Instead of practicing medicine, physicians are instead are forced to chase statistics and numbers.

CUSTOMER SERVICE

Every physician should have a good bedside manner. They should speak to their patients professionally and calmly, discuss the risks and benefits of various treatments, and be pleasant and professional. They should be understanding, compassionate, and caring. They should answer their patients' questions. However, physicians should *not* be rated for their "customer service" or "patient satisfaction."

Typically, patient satisfaction is measured by surveys after a patient visits a provider. These surveys ask if you liked your physician, if they were friendly, if they treated your pain, if you waited too long, etc. The theory is that higher scores are given by those who liked their care. The scores range from 1–5 (or strongly agree to strongly disagree), with five being the best. With the passage of the Affordable Healthcare Act in 2010, physicians and hospitals rated lower were paid less than those with higher scores. Hospitals and people like money, and thus a larger focus is placed on patient satisfaction.

This pursuit of patient satisfaction was placed into practice with the best of intentions. It makes sense that you should treat pain and be nice to the patient. But the nature of medicine makes it nearly impossible to have patients give you high scores consistently, and patient satisfaction scores have become a nightmare to deal with. Patients have expectations of what should happen and how they should be medically treated. But what they think should happen is not always the best medical treatment. In some cases, it might even harm the patient.

Let's imagine a really common scenario. A patient comes in with cold symptoms. They want antibiotics. You know antibiotics are not indicated for simple viral infections. You speak to the patient at length and answer all their questions. They understand, leave, and when they get home, they write a review. They write something like: "I gave the doctor a 3 out of 5 because, while she was nice, she did not give me antibiotics." You took the time to explain to the patient that there is a high chance their infection is viral. You told the patient about antibiotic side effects and increasing antibiotic resistance. But no matter, you did not meet the patient's expectations of being given antibiotics, and thus your score is low.

"Well, okay," you might tell yourself, "I don't care about scores, they don't matter." Well, guess again. You better believe administration will be on your case about it. They might have someone follow you around to see how you act or recommend additional education. Poor patient satisfaction affects the bottom line, and we all know that is the health-care system's priority.

Wanting to get high patient satisfaction scores might cause you to change the way you practice. You might prescribe more antibiotics or pain medicines just so you can get a higher score and administration will leave you alone. One physician is suing her employer for this very reason [6]. She claims she was incentivized to prescribe more opioid prescriptions to get higher patient-satisfaction scores. If true, this is not good medicine. A large study has found that pursuing patient satisfaction leads to increased mortality and higher healthcare costs [7].

I'm not saying a physician should be a rude jerk who has no compassion for anyone and finds medicine to be eternal torment. But a physician visit is not the same as going to a restaurant, staying at a hotel, or seeing a concert. And yet the practice of rating, which is more becoming more common, has many implications. It can affect pay, for example. In one article, physician salaries in some cases directly to patient satisfaction surveys [8]. If patients do not "like" the physician, he'll get paid less.

In medicine, the patient cannot always get what they want. No matter how good your bedside manner, there will always be those who rate you low for reasons outside of your control, and there is nothing you can do about it.

NON-CLINICAL PERSONNEL

In many states, corporations cannot own a physician practice. Laws prohibiting this were enacted ostensibly to prevent corporations from taking over and telling a physician what they should and should not do. However, enforcement of these laws are lax at best, any many loopholes exist for corporations and private investors to "run" the business side of a practice. It may be a surprise to know (well, maybe not if you've read this far) that there are ways that corporations and personnel do in fact control physicians.

Take for example, a private equity group that runs a dermatology practice. They might push the physicians to sell a particular product that they get a higher commission for, even if it is inferior or not the recommended treatment. They may try and get their physicians to do more biopsies or other procedures, knowing that it makes them more money. Business people are telling doctors, in essence, how to practice medicine.

Consider a real-life example. Dr. Good was recently discharging a patient with a complicated illness from the hospital.[4] During discharge, he took the time to discuss with the patient any concerns they might have. The patient understood and thanked the doctor for his care. But on the survey given to all patients, the patient wrote that while she liked the doctor, she was a little confused about some of her diabetic medications (even though all questions were answered).

An administrator notices this and decides that customer satisfaction is not as high as it could have been. This administrator, who is not a physician (and does not hold any medical degree, for that matter) emails the medical director and all executive staff to say that Dr. Good needs "remediation" and sends a document describing what Dr. Good should do when it comes to managing diabetes. Dr. Good is appalled. What went wrong? Didn't he try to do everything right?

The administrator has no idea what it is really like to practice medicine. There was not a bad clinical outcome. The administrator simply looks at some numbers, and instead of trying to determine what actually happened, immediately blames the physician.

It's not that there is just an occasional bad administrator either. Many administrators will try and tell you how to do your job without really understanding what it is about. When a score here or there might be low, it doesn't matter what really happened. Context is irrelevant.

If you're a physician, all of this might make you feel you're a cog in the machine. Indeed, one physician told me she feels like an "Uber Doc." You don't control how many patients you want to see or how many days you work. You come to the practice to make money for the hospital or investor group. You have to please your patients instead of doing what's best for them. And if you break down, they will replace you.

MENTAL HEALTH AND PHYSICIAN SUICIDE

In America, about one physician a day is lost to suicide [9]. This is double the rate of the regular population, which is about 28–40 per 100,000 [10]. Physicians have some of the highest risk of death by suicide when compared to all other occupations. One study found that physicians kill themselves at a higher rate than soldiers [11].

Why are physicians at greater risk of committing suicide? Many studies have attempted to discover the reason, but to me the answer is obvious: Medical school and residency are grueling experiences. The demands tax a person's mind and body. The hours are long, the sleep nonexistent, the pressures sometimes insurmountable. Combine this with the stigma people who feel suicidal can face when going for help, and one can begin to understand why.

It is often too difficult, as a physician, to seek out help for depression or other mental health issues. A physician is supposed to be seen as "resilient." In residency, the long hours are supposed to "build character." Patient care is number one—your own health and well-being come later, if ever. Sacrifice, sacrifice, and sacrifice. That is the duty of a physician, and if you fail at this task you are no physician at all.

If your colleagues or your supervisor find out that you are struggling, they may question your competency. In medical school and residency, this means being pulled off of rotations, which may push back your graduation date. You may have to undergo a psychiatric evaluation. (Indeed, a colleague who reached out for help was not allowed back until they were cleared by a psychiatrist). And, usually, when one person knows what happened, the whole class does. Once the cat is out of the bag, it's hard to get it back in.

It is no wonder, then, that physicians might not seek help. The consequences for reaching out are too high. Do you want to be known as the "weak" resident who couldn't take it? There are questions about mental health are on most state medical license applications! If you struggled during residency or medical school, you may feel you're being penalized.

Once you become an attending, one form of stress replaces another. Most are out of the physicians' control. Administration will hound you. You spend hours documenting. Your hospital is chronically understaffed and some of your patients can be quite rude. You may even be attacked or killed [12]. Sometimes it adds up and can be depressing.

The COVID-19 pandemic happens, and the stressors increase by ten-fold. You try your best, but you are powerless against a never-ending stream of critical patients. Sometimes these stressors are too much, and they tragically take the life of other physicians [13].

While in recent years there may be a renewed focus on the mental health of physicians and medical staff, in my opinion, it is far too little. There is a very real risk of suicide or other mental health issues in medicine. If physician suicide is to be addressed, we must re-examine exactly what we do to people who go through the process of training. We must also examine the very real stressors practicing physicians face, and realize that *we* are patients as well. In my opinion, physicians cannot sacrifice everything, including their lives, for medicine. That is not a sustainable model.

INSURANCE COMPANIES AND MANDATES

Insurance companies can be one of the biggest pains in your bottom to deal with. Prior Authorizations. Denied coverage. Rising premiums, while at the same time covering less. Do you want to treat a patient's asthma by giving them a prescription for an inhaled steroid? Too bad, the insurance company won't cover it. You need to go with this other, inferior treatment first. Want to do a diagnostic test? Make sure insurance covers it, and in some cases get prior authorization. To deal with the insurance companies and their denials day after day wears you down. It might make you think that they're only in it for the money (hmm). How many times have you heard of someone having to fight an insurance company? How many times has your physician had to fight with the insurance company? It's practically taken for granted at this point.

If that isn't bad enough, consider how much power the

insurance company really wields. Imagine a future where you are a fully-fledged physician. You've reached the top. You'd like to prescribe certain treatments and examine patients on a schedule that is convenient to them and your-self. Well, wait just one minute! The insurance company demands that you practice medicine a certain way. You can be open only on specific days. Think this is fiction? Guess again. A pediatrician wrote an article about how an insur-ance auditor told her what she could and could not do [14].

The short version of the story is this: The physician wanted to give vaccines to kids. Kids under nine must be immunized by a physician in Washington State. Many parents scheduled an annual checkup and the vaccine at the same time. The insurance company didn't like that (the theory being it is more expensive for the insurance company, decreasing their bottom line). They told the physician not to do that, and not to run her clinic on Saturdays. When the pediatrician did not agree, she was reported to the State Medical Board for going against "an insurance company mandate." Just think about it: You work all your life to become a medical professional. You study and believe you're helping the community at large. Then the insurance company comes around and tells you what to do and what not to do. Essentially, an entity without a medical license tells you how to practice medicine. And it's legal! What can you do? They're bigger than you. They make hundreds of millions of dollars in profit. They can bring you down if they feel like it. They can tell you what to do and leave you trying to fix everything in the aftermath. Sounds like a great deal, right?

This particular physician had to fork over $8,000 in legal fees to clear her name. Sounds fair, doesn't it? They don't prepare you for that in medical school.

Not only is this a problem for physicians, but it is also

one for the patient population at large. Remember, insurance companies are usually after one thing: profit. They will make decisions time and time again to make money. Don't think so? Let's take a look at the net income of the top four insurance companies in the USA over the first quarter of 2019:

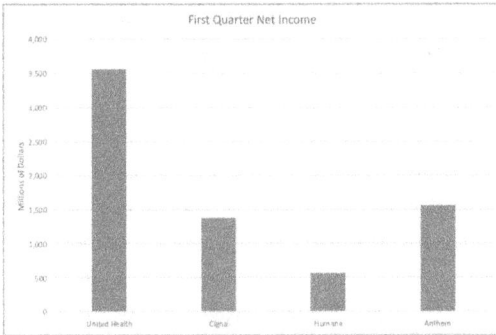

And that's in *MILLIONS* of dollars. Millions. In the first three months of 2019, United Healthgroup made $3,557,000,000 in net income [15]. That's almost $4 billion dollars in three months. In three months. Just imagine going against that. How could you? You are essentially nothing to them. You have a medical degree, true. Good for you, I guess. But they have billions of dollars. It's not worth the headache.

Every healthcare dollar spent on healthcare administration is, in my opinion, a failure of the healthcare industry.

HOSPITAL GROUPS AND PRIVATE EQUITY

You see it more and more: Physicians are working for either private equity or large hospital systems. Private equity, where a group of private investors buy out a practice and "run" the management side, has been rapidly expanding throughout the healthcare field. Just take a look at the field of dermatology, for example, to get an idea of how prevalent it is. In 2012, there were only five private equity acquisitions in this field. In 2017, there were 59 [16].

Typically, the goal of private equity is to buy out a certain practice or company, take over the management, and increase profit. Then, they attempt to sell the practice for profit in about 3–5 years. Theoretically, private equity will take care of the business side of things in a practice and leave the physician to take care of the medicine side. Private equity also gives a large paycheck to the physician when buying out a practice.

In reality, things can be very different. How does a private equity company increase profit? Well, typically in a business, you cut costs and raise prices. Private equity works the same way. Although the physician selling the practice might get a large paycheck, other physicians in the group may see their pay lowered by 30% or more. Physicians may be fired altogether and be replaced by mid-level providers to lower costs. Private equity might "recommend" employing certain treatments when not needed or recommend the sale of certain products.

For example, an article in the *New York Times* describes the controversy involved with private equity firms [17]. The article recounts the story of a dermatologist who submitted a paper to a journal describing the financial impact private equity firms have had on medical practices. The doctor's paper described how patients' costs went up after dermatology practices were acquired by private equity. Private equity firms, of course, were angry. After numerous calls and letters, the original paper was retracted because of "factual errors." It remains unpublished to this day.

Another example is a recent settlement the Department of Justice made with large physician staffing groups in 2017 [18]. There, the companies were found at fault for admitting patients to the hospital for unnecessary work up and exams.

This was done in an effort to apparently bring up the bill for patients and insurers to pay.

Now, not every private equity firm acts like this. Anyone can point to firms who do not do these things. But you cannot deny that at the end of the day, private equity is after money, while you went into medicine to, you know, help people.

Like it or not, corporate medicine seems to be rapidly expanding. Today, the top two physician staffing companies employ over 41,000 clinicians. Hospitals in almost all of the contiguous United States are contracted by these two. Chances are, if you are in emergency medicine, anesthesiology, orthopedics, or ambulatory surgery (or others!), you will run into these companies.

HOSPITAL SYSTEMS

If you don't work for private equity, you might work for a hospital or hospital system. Hospital systems are increasingly and rapidly consolidating, with over 100 acquisitions in 2015, 2016, and 2017 [19]. Hospital consolidations share similar problems with large equity groups: If they dominate your area, you don't have much choice in who to work for; they might lower your pay; and they might subject you to onerous administrative tasks and tracking.

One of the largest for-profit hospital systems in the United States, the Hospital Corporation of America (HCA), cut the salary of physicians, nurses, and staff during the COVID-19 pandemic [20]. Physicians and staff continued to work long hours, get sick, and sacrifice everything while getting paid less. In July 2020, HCA reported a 1.1 billion-dollar *net profit* in the midst of the pandemic [21]. The company essentially profited off of the health crisis. They claim that their CEO donated two months of his salary to assist those employees in need. This is technically true. However, accounting for stock compensation, bonuses, etc., this comes out to be less than 1% of his annual $26 million in compensation [20]. The front-line physicians and staff risk their lives, while those at the top of large hospital systems enrich themselves.

For profit and non-for-profit hospital systems typically pay their executives extraordinary amounts in compensation. It's easy to see what can happen when money is involved. Profits and shareholders are prioritized. Patients, physicians, and the healthcare system are not. In my opinion, business people should have no say when it comes to medicine.

THE PHARMACEUTICAL INDUSTRY AND YOU

Valeant Pharmaceuticals raised the price of a drug (penicillamine) to treat Wilson's disease from $652 to $21,267 in 2015 [22]. In 2009, an EpiPen was about $100, costing $600 in 2016 [23]. In 1923, the inventor of insulin, Frederick Banting, sold the patent to the University of Toronto for a mere $1. In 2016, the monthly price of insulin was about $450 [24].

The pharmaceutical companies can try and explain it away any way they want, but numbers don't lie, and prices for medications have been rising at a ridiculous rate. Being a physician means indirectly facilitating the behavior of these large corporations. If a patient needs medicine for Wilson's disease, diabetes, or some other illness, you *have* to prescribe it. For certain diseases, there might be only one or two medications you can prescribe. These might be very costly (like penicillamine). You don't want to facilitate pharmaceutical companies' exorbitant price-gouging, but your hands are tied, as the patient needs this expensive medication.

Unfortunately, when you're the only game in town and the patients need the drug, well, they're going to pay.

Even if it shouldn't be this way, you, the physician, are fattening the pockets of the CEOs and pharmacy benefit managers with the patient's literal life savings. All you wanted to do was treat somebody. Now you are part of this literal life-or-death game and there is nothing you can do about it. Sure, the companies have "drug assistance programs," but these programs have complicated applications and requirements, and their benefits are often unclear due to a lack of transparency [25]. You could try physician activism, like when the American College of Physicians wrote a paper recommending lowering drug prices [26]. But most physicians (in my personal experience) are more concerned with finishing their work and getting home.

All in all, the trend is scary: Corporations and the pursuit of profit are bad for healthcare; you, the hopeful physician, are little more than a cog in the machine; the patients often have poorer outcomes; and the bottom-line increases.

SUMMARY

Physicians are subject to a host of non-clinical duties, which can cause them to feel "burned-out." It is an inevitable by-product of working in a healthcare system that prioritizes profit over patient.

- A whopping 44% of physicians are "burned out."
- Physicians document too much, and the EMR used for charting is slow and inefficient.
- Administration tracks physicians and how they manage patients. They may tell physicians how to practice though they have no medical degree.

- Government regulations are onerous and unnecessary.
- Patients may rate physicians poorly even if they have done everything right medically.
- Insurance companies are powerful and may tell physicians how to practice medicine.
- Private equity and hospitals systems are focused on trying to maximize profits. This may come at the expense of the patient and the physician.
- Physicians might have to prescribe expensive medications and contribute to increasing healthcare costs.

3

MALPRACTICE

Imagine that in the summer of your young hopeful college years you dream of becoming a doctor. "I want to help people!" you exclaim. Your eyes, bright and full of life, look at the college campus life around you. You know it will be a long journey, but it will be worth it! You will directly make a difference in people's lives and in the community around you.

You study. Day after day, month after month, you spend your time reading. While others play, you read. The library is your closest friend. You pass the MCAT (even though you think the essay part is stupid). You get into the medical school of your choice.

Medical school is long and expensive. The years go by. You spend more of your life indoors than out. The exams are difficult, the curriculum grueling. And, while you have your ups and downs in school, finally, you graduate and move into your number one residency spot.

While the number of loans slowly grows to over $300,000, you start to get paid! A small salary, but it's better than nothing! Residency is even tougher than medical school. Your hair starts to gray. But you keep your bright smile and stick with it. Eventually, you graduate from that too! By this point, you have invested at least 11 years of your life and over three hundred thousand dollars (it turns out the payments that you have been making in residency don't even cover the interest payments, so your debt increases).

Finally, you are an attending! Life and medicine are yours to command! No more annoying attendings above you. You can do whatever you want! You can practice however you choose! Sure, there are politics, but you get paid the big bucks!

You are making $200,000+! You don't know what to do with the money.

One day at work, you have a difficult case. You try your best. You get consultants, specialists, and almost everyone on board. The patient suffers complications.

You get served a lawsuit. You read the headlines. But you already know what happened. You were there in the courtroom.

You received a judgment against you for $110 million dollars [27]. Or $229 million dollars [28]. Or $178 million dollars [29].

Gee, being a doctor sure is great, isn't it? Good luck trying to pay that back.

Medical malpractice is the dreaded complication of being a physician. About 1 in 3 of all physicians are sued [30]. One questionable mistake may cost you very big bucks. Years and years of studying won't cover all the cash. For example, the salary of an average critical care doctor is about $324k a year. Even if they worked *another 30 years* (and you have to be young to do that), they would only make about 9.7 million dollars. They could work for the rest of their lives and never cover the bill.

Malpractice insurance will cover it, you think to yourself.

If the hospital was also part of the lawsuit, the physician might not be on the hook for all of it. The defendants will also likely appeal, and the amount awarded will likely be lowered to something more reasonable. Even so, would you go to a physician who had a $110 million-dollar verdict against him?

These examples portray a common theme in malpractice: You are judged by lay persons, not medical peers. Say what you will about the judicial system, in the end, juries may be swayed by a good enough story to award the plaintiff damages, even if you are entirely in the clear. In France, as you'll see later, things are different. The malpractice cases go to courts that consist of medical professionals, and any judgments are paid by the state. While that solution might be difficult to implement here, it is clear that medicine cannot continue down its current path. It is simply unsustainable. If enough doctors are sued by their patients, who will practice medicine?

Sometimes you may be sued even if you do not make the mistake yourself. Most physicians are expected to sign the charts of physician assistants or nurse practitioners who work with them. If you trust the PA or NP and blindly sign their chart, beware. You may find yourself on the receiving end of a lawsuit. It may be better to briefly examine the patients they see, check, edit and add to their note. Nothing is foolproof, however.

With one lawsuit, you get placed into the National Practitioner Data Bank (NPDB). This data bank tracks successful lawsuits (and other adverse actions such as settlements) a physician might have. Not only are you in this database, but you must also report the lawsuit on *all* of your future job applications and medical board applications. You will likely carry this albatross around your neck forever.

Many malpractice suits are settled before they go to trial.

While this might be cheaper for you and your insurer, you still get placed into the NPDB.[1] These settlements may also come with the caveat that you admit wrongdoing, even if you treated the patient perfectly.

No one goes to medical school or into medicine for the purpose of harming someone. But should one error, usually out of your control, threaten an entire career? Humans are imperfect by nature. Things happen. There needs to be a better solution to malpractice, and this is not it.

Consider the way that law is practiced by a judge. Judges cannot be sued for the verdicts they deliver [31]. The law says a judge should be protected because, if they are sued for a verdict, the way that they practice law might change. Imagine if you could sue a judge because you didn't like what they decided. Every judge would be sued! Unfortunately, this is not the case in medicine. Do you think the physicians who had the $110 million-dollar verdict against them will practice medicine the same way? Of course not. They will practice something called "defensive medicine" (or as I like to call it, cover-your-ass medicine). More tests. More unnecessary workups, which can actually worsen clinical outcomes. If they even continue to practice at all, that is.

It was constantly said in residency: "You are not smarter than a CT scan!" And indeed, that is true. Unfortunately, physicians are punished for missing the diagnosis, even when the diagnosis is very hard or impossible to come by in the first place. Some scary diagnoses can be subtle and missed by even the best of physicians and the most thorough of exams. Clinical judgment can be easily misled. It is difficult to be a physician, and early in your hopeful career you will realize that it is impossible to catch everything.

Yes, sometimes physicians are wrong, and patients have bad outcomes. And sometimes care is negligent. But in a typical malpractice case, is it fair to be penalized severely?

SUMMARY

In the course of practicing medicine, the law may be something you have to face. Malpractice is the dreaded complication of practicing medicine.

- About 1 in 3 of all physicians are sued.
- Some verdicts can be tremendously expensive.
- If you settle or lose a lawsuit, your name will be placed in the National Practitioner Data Bank.
- You may be sued from signing PA or NP charts.
- You might be sued even if the diagnosis was impossible to get right.

4

TIME AND MONEY

The average time from deciding to be a physician to actually being an attending (a fully-fledged physician) varies according to what specialty one goes into. Let's imagine you want to take the time to become a physician. What would your process look like?

To become a physician in the U.S., you would have to start in college (sometimes even in high school). You are excited about becoming a doctor. Science! Helping people! All sounds great. A freshman in college, you look online and see the following requirements to be a pre-medical student:

• Two semesters of biology with laboratory (up to four semesters at some schools)
• Two semesters of inorganic chemistry with laboratory
• Two semesters of organic chemistry with laboratory
• Two semesters of math, at least one in calculus
• Two semesters of physics with laboratory
• Two semesters of English and/or writing

OK, you think to yourself, there's some random math and chemistry in there that physicians probably don't use (or do they??!) but sounds good otherwise.[1] Let's get the process started!

So, you begin. You read, and study, and read. You take your tests. But it's not enough just to pass the subjects. Medical schools are very competitive in the U.S., and the closer you are to that sweet 4.0 GPA, the better your chances are of getting in. About 65% of applicants with a GPA over 3.79 are accepted to medical school; only 32% are accepted with a GPA between 3.4 and 3.59, regardless of their MCAT scores [32]. You study like crazy. Hours and hours and hours are spent indoors, reading, studying, trying to get the information down.

You reach your third year. Your eventual goal is to take the MCAT (Medical College Admissions Test), which will let you get into medical school. You study for crazy like that as well.

During your final years of college, you are only about 1/3 done with your training (having completed four out of a total of 11 to 12 years). You haven't even started actual clinical work yet. Someone pursuing a different career (finance, accounting, etc.) might be very close to the end. They might also pay significantly less in schooling overall.

Unfortunately, you may not have the money to pay for college. Like the other 44 million Americans who can't afford college, you decide to take out a loan. But you are very special and get to take out a *student* loan, one that cannot be discharged in bankruptcy.

In 2019, the average cost of a four-year undergraduate degree was a whopping $87,800.[2] For out of state students, the cost balloons to $153,320 [33]. While you can take out some federal loans that are subsidized (meaning the government pays the interest while you are in school), the rest of the loan gains interest. Even then, there is a maximum to what the government will lend you as an undergraduate;[3] the rest will have to come from private loans or your own pocket.

Assuming you take out an unsubsidized loan, your interest rate will be 6.08% in 2020 [34]. There is also a 1.060% fee that is deducted proportionally from each disbursement of the loan. Simplifying things, a loan of $87,800 at a 6.08% interest rate will cost you $29,594 in interest over 10 years. That assumes you will be paying it off after college, and not letting it accumulate even more interest while you're in medical school.

One might argue that with a physician's salary the loan is easier to pay. The average salary among all specialties for a doctor is about $313,000 [35]. That shouldn't take too long to pay off, right?

Yes, a physician's salary will help in paying off the loan. However, a college student who transitions directly into medical school doesn't stop to repay their loans; they usually place them into deferment and add more debt. While it might seem like the total amount you pay back can be easily found through the use of online student loan calculators, it is actually larger, as no payments are being made for 8 years instead of just 4 (4 years of college plus 4 years of medical school). That loan you said you would pay in 10 years is a loan that you *let collect* interest for 8 years and then started to pay. We all hear about the power of compounding interest. If you add on graduate school, the total student loan debt is even higher. Some physicians in their fifties are *still* paying off their loans. Adding medical school increases your debt burden even further.

If your passion for medical school is high, but your GPA isn't high enough, one thing you can do is go into graduate school to raise it. The theory is that your graduate GPA is calculated from graduate courses only and not from the undergraduate ones. So, if you didn't do well in some of your courses, a fresh start with a graduate GPA might be the way to go. However, your wallet will take the hit. For graduate school, the government will not provide you with subsidized loans. Only unsubsidized loans or PLUS loans are available. The school itself is expensive. The typical cost of a one-year graduate program in the U.S. is a whopping $20,000! This is nearly half the cost of a 4-year undergraduate program, and it is for one year of graduate school only. The cost goes up every year you stay on. The debt and time commitment only increase.

For some people, even getting paid in residency doesn't cover the compounding monthly interest they accumulate on their loan. For example, consider a medical school debt of roughly $260,000 (with more than $50,000 in interest). The interest rate when this loan was taken out was a whopping 6.8%. Every month, the medical school loan increased about $1,500—and this was just in pure interest. In residency, your payments might be only about $300 every month. This is because the payments are calculated on your salary. However, even though you are "making payments" on your loans, the actual debt keeps on going higher. After the payments, your loan would still increase by $1,200 *every month* (There goes your stimulus check). You will pay off a little interest, but the debt increases. Luckily, there are forgiveness programs (public forgiveness and taxable forgiveness after 25 years), but these programs carry the risk of changing their terms or being eliminated altogether. This is not every case, but it is a *real-life* case, so consider something similar if loans are for you.

You might say money isn't everything. Even though your net worth might be negative for a while, eventually, you'll pay able to pay it off. But how about the cost of something more valuable, something that you can never get back?

The time commitment to becoming a fully-fledged physician in the U.S. is crazy. Typically, including college, it is about 11 years. Eleven years! It took Jeff Bezos *7 years* to have Amazon turn its first profit (and even then, it took so long only because it *re-invested* its profits in itself first).[4] It took Microsoft *7 years*, from its conception to the release of Microsoft Windows, to turn its shareholders into billionaires and millionaires. Being a physician takes *at least* 11 years (not considering special combined programs), and during this time, you are in *debt*! (unless you are very lucky). Your net worth is negative for some years after you become an attending. Yes, yes, I know. Companies are different than your path to medicine. Not every company is even successful. 11 years is still a long time though. If you did not choose medicine, who knows what you would be able to accomplish?

Interestingly, the process of becoming a physician is different overseas. In France, anyone who finishes high school can apply to medical school, merely after taking an admissions test [36]! That skips a potential *4 years* of expensive schooling that you would otherwise do in the U.S. And if you think that high school in France covers a different age group than it is in the U.S., you would be wrong! High school (*lycée*) is from the ages of 15–18, as in the United States. If you also believe that the French health system produces inferior doctors due to a lack time spent in school, you would be wrong again. According to a World Health Organization study, France was found to have overall the best healthcare system in the world, followed by Italy, Spain, and others [37]. The U.S., by comparison, is number 37, lower than Colombia and the United Arab Emirates. Looking at the way the U.S. handled the 2020 Coronavirus pandemic confirms this.

Not only do you spend less time becoming a doctor in France, but the cost of medical school is government subsidized. If you do not realize the amazingness of completely paid-for medical school, let me say it again: Medical school in France is almost completely *free* (yes, taxes in France are higher; see below). The boatload of debt that comes with college and medical school in the United States just does not happen in France. The average cost of medical school in the United States (which we will discuss below) is a whopping $183,000 in the U.S., with typical repayments ranging from $329,000 to $480,000 [38]. The art of loaning potential physicians money is lucrative, is it not?

Of course, one can say that physicians in France get paid less than their American counterparts. Taxes are much higher as well, so it is not a true comparison. (How can you compare one healthcare system to another?) And this is true. A physician in France might make about $92,000 as a primary care doctor and maybe around $150,000 as a specialist. Compare this to the average of about $195,000 for primary care and $284,000 for specialists in the U.S. [35]. However, there are some important caveats to consider. For one, as mentioned, the cost of medical school is zero in France, whereas a U.S. based physician has to pay back staggering loans. This makes the net worth of a U.S.-based physician negative compared to a positive net worth of someone in France (assuming they had no debts when going into medical school). Two, the gross domestic product per capita is about 20% less in France than it is in the U.S., so everyone earns a little less there. Also, as mentioned, malpractice works very differently in France, so that doctors are not weighed down by potential malpractice-related costs (insurance, court costs, lawyers, etc.)

In France, malpractice cases are decided by special review boards that operate outside the court system. The malpractice award is also paid by a national fund, so physicians are free from the exorbitant costs of malpractice insurance. Indeed, in the U.S., according to one American Medical Association (AMA) report, obstetric and gynecological physicians pay anywhere from $30,000—$200,000 in malpractice insurance alone [39]. Payouts in France are also lower. There are no malpractice payouts of hundreds of millions of dollars.

The point is this: In the end, you might get paid less in France as a doctor, but in the U.S., you're paying with the currency of time, future earnings, potential lawsuits, and insurance.

Now, the financial aspect of medicine is appealing, and depending on what specialty you go into, you can make quite a bit of money. In 2019, specialties like orthopedics made about $482,000 on average a year and cardiology about $430,000 [35]. This amount of money is more than enough to bring you up to speed in a couple of years. But that is typically if you specialize. If your interest is in pediatrics or family medicine, you won't make as much. In 2019, pediatrics was one of the lowest-paid specialties, coming in at $225,000, and family practice at $231,000. You'll still live comfortably at this level, but it will take you longer to pay off any loans you have, in addition to doing normal "grown-up" stuff, like buying a house or saving for retirement. As an attending, you'll have to live like a resident for a couple of years in order to get some of those things.

PHYSICIAN ASSISTANTS AND NURSE PRACTITIONERS

By 2030, estimates show a shortage of between 46,900 and 121,900 physicians [40]. The number of primary care physicians lacking is estimated to be from 21,100 to 55,200. This will inevitability lead to lack of care, with rural areas especially hard hit.

In some states, such as Florida, the solution has been to allow advance-practice registered nurses, such as nurse practitioners (NPs) and physician assistants (PAs) to practice independently [41]. Physician groups, of course, were not happy about this. They argued that this might lower the quality of care given to patients and cause more errors. Nurse practitioners and PAs disagreed.

The point is not to discuss whether physicians or PAs and NPs are qualified. But, if they can practice independently in family practice and other fields, what is the point of spending the time and money necessary to be a physician? Physician assistants go through college and they then spend two to three years in PA school. Afterward, they can practice medicine independently if they meet state requirements.[5] Advance practice registered nurses (APRNs) are similar. If you go the standard route, you may go to school and become an APRN in 6 years or less. Compare this with a physician, who typically goes to school for a minimum of 11 years. Why spend the time and money training to be a physician when there is another cheaper and faster option? Physicians get paid more, but as discussed below, they also are the dictionary definition of delayed gratification.

SUMMARY

In the end, you will pay to be a physician with time and a lot of money. A lot of your time will be spent learning; you will be the embodiment of delayed gratification. But the time you have already paid out still isn't enough; the years of residency await you.

- The medical school application process is very competitive.
- The cost of college and medical school is very expensive.
- You'll spend many years training to be a physician.

- If you take out loans, you may not be able to pay them back for a long time. During this time the interest adds up, and you will be in hundreds of thousands of dollars in debt by the time you graduate.
- PA's and NP's go through less schooling and more states are allowing them to practice on their own.

5

RESIDENCY

S o, you made it through medical school. The tests were tough, but you got through them. Now it's time for residency. You've seen *ER* and *The Resident*. Well, I'm sorry to inform you, it's not exactly like that.

You are interested in surgery. You match into a surgical residency. You enjoy working with your hands. You think it's cool that you will get to operate, as you get a chance to directly and visibly influence someone's life.

You work long hours, about 80–100 hours a week. Every three days you have to stay at the hospital for 24 hours ("on call"). Life changes dramatically. All you know is work. Most of the time, as a first-year resident, you are not even operating; your seniors have you do other, more menial tasks ("scut work"). You begin to question your decisions.

While surgical residency is more difficult than most, whatever residency you're in, you will still be working quite a bit. All physicians regularly work long hours, and residents even longer. Consider the term "resident." Why would you call a physician in training a "resident"? The answer is simple: they live at the hospital. They wake up at the hospital.

They eat, sleep, and shower at the hospital. Just as one is a resident of one's home or apartment, so is a training physician a "resident" of the hospital.

Residency is challenging. Often, these long hours will have detrimental effects on your physical and mental health and may even affect patient care.

In 1984, Libby Zion died at the hands of two overworked resident physicians on a 36-hour shift. She was administered a medication that caused something called "serotonin syndrome," leading to cardiac arrest and death. After a long trial and investigation, the Bell Commission was eventually established. It set limits on resident working hours and was adopted by New York State and later by the Accreditation Council for Graduate Medical Education (ACGME nationally in 2003 [42]).[1] It sets hours on resident work, as outlined below:

1. An 80-hour-week limit, averaged over one month
2. Eight hours off duty between shifts
3. A 14-hour period free from clinical work after a 24-hour in-house call shift[2]
4. A 24-hour limit on a resident's shift (but this can be extended to 30 hours for "education" and continuity of care)
5. No new patients after 24 hours on duty
6. One day free of all physician duties and education every 7 days (averaged over one month)
7. Residents may not be on at-home call[3] more than every third night averaged over a month

The rules were needed; but as is often the case, real life is different. It is common knowledge among the surgical residency program at many hospitals that reporting the *actual* number of hours worked is heavily frowned upon. Why? If the hours reported are more than what is allowed, well, the ACGME does not exactly like that. They will come down hard, in some cases closing the residency program.

A surgical resident physician I worked with told me how the trauma service was run. Typically, his day began at 4 am and ended at midnight. He would wake up and "round" on all the patients.[4] Usually, there were about 40–50 patients on the service. Then, he would have to manage the incoming trauma patients. Some of these would be very critical—for example, gunshot wounds and stabbings. He told me he would be lucky to get sleep. His attending was at the hospital, but his contribution would be nothing more than eyeballing the patient and asking the patient if they wanted to be discharged. This is a vastly unsafe practice. Too high a workload and lack of sleep and supervision can have disastrous results for patient care. It just doesn't work, as was already discovered in 1984.

My friend told me he would often work over 120 hours a week. At one point, he confided in me that this was destroying him, and he just wanted to quit medicine. I didn't know what to tell him. Imagine, working and studying all those years, and incurring all that debt, just to be burned out by unfair and unsafe work conditions. And if you quit, well how are you going to pay back your $200k+ of loans? It is not a decision I wish on anyone.

If you think it is as simple as reporting this to the ACGME, guess again. Not only did my friend feel the pressure of other senior residents telling him not to report it, but whistleblowers have no protection under the ACGME. If he had reported this program, his own residency would be in jeopardy. The ACGME would have likely cracked down on the program, but the end effect would likely have been to shut the program down entirely. You can see how this would be a problem. He would be out of a job. Transferring to another program is an option, of course, but usually the programs that accept transfers are less than ideal. Time would be lost as well. Instead of graduating on time, his graduation would have been pushed back months.

The medical community is smaller than you think. Word of mouth travels quickly. If he was outed as the resident who brought down a program, do you think programs would be more likely to take him on? They would see him as a risk. He might not get a job at all.

Unfortunately, residents in this position are left with just two options: quit or do it. My friend chose the latter, but to this day he does not appear to have the same zest for medicine that he once had.

OTHER LONG SHIFTS

In residency, and maybe as an attending, you will often be subject to 24-hour or 36-hour shifts. The reasoning is that if you spend 24 hours with the patient, there will be better "continuity of care." You know the patient, you should be able to better manage them.

Have you ever tried to stay up 24–36 hours? How about while working? Your cognition starts to suffer. Your decision-making suffers. Yet you may still need to make life-and-death decisions. Do you want your pilot flying for 36 hours straight? So why, why, would anyone think that your physician being awake for that many hours is a good idea?

Yes, yes, I know what other physicians might say. "Patient care might suffer," (ignoring the fact you've been awake for 36 hours). "More errors occur during the transfer of patient care," they say. That's a non-answer. In my opinion, there is really no reason for 24- or 36-hour shifts. If there is a way patient care "may" suffer, then find a way around it! How is it possible all the physicians and their groups combined can't come up with a solution to this?

ONE-SIDED CONTRACTS

I wished they had said more in residency about contracts offered to you when applying for an attending job. These contracts are only minimally discussed, leaving opportunities to take advantage of a new attending. Always, always, always negotiate your contract and have a lawyer review it. Most new attendings have no idea what a good contract is. Often, they end up signing restrictive, employer-friendly contracts. The language is often confusing and opaque, which benefits the company.

Some of the more standard clauses are discussed below. Get them out of your contract as soon as you can.

GEOGRAPHICAL RESTRICTIONS

Ahh, the geographical restriction. This is a typical clause, not only in the medical field but in many other fields. The clause basically says that if you quit, you can't work within a certain number of miles of your old job. Usually, it's something like 5–20 miles, but I've seen some contracts stipulate up to 50. The theory is that they don't want you to work for their competitor.

This restriction might make sense until you begin to look at exactly where other practice groups are. They're usually all within 50 miles! Signing one of these contracts means if you live in a town that has two practices, one right next to the other, and you quit, you can't work for the other guy. That means you then have to travel to the next place, which can be far away. And some of these contracts last for 2 years! Do you really want to drive 1 ½ hours every time you go to work for the next 2 years?

If you can strike it out, then do it. California residents are lucky because non-compete clauses are unenforceable in the state (though those companies may still put it in the contract for some reason).

MALPRACTICE COVERAGE

Any good company that hires physicians should cover your malpractice insurance. Even if it's a private group, there should still be coverage. Ideally, you'd like something called occurrence-based coverage. Occurrence-based coverage means that the insurer will cover you whenever a lawsuit may arise from your practice, even if you quit your job years ago. The only downside is that it's more expensive, but I think it's worth it.

Compare this with claims-made insurance, which is way more common (it's cheaper). Most physicians will have this policy. This policy covers you only if it is in effect when a lawsuit happens. You're only covered where you work. Say you got sued for telling the patient they only had a cold when in reality they had a brain bleed. If the policy was in effect, you would be covered. Say they sued you again but the policy was not in effect because you had left the job to try your hand at professional poker playing. You would be on the hook for everything yourself.

You can see why this is a problem. If you quit, your coverage ends. Most of the time, lawsuits happen years later. So, what do you do? Why, purchase a "tail", of course. A tail covers you after you leave a place. In my opinion, the company hiring you should pay for it. A tail means that if you were sued after you left, you would still be covered by the insurance. You should always try and get the company you work for to pay for your tail. They can be expensive if purchased yourself.

BENEFITS

If you're an employee, try to get some benefits: health insurance, continuing medical education (CME) allowance, paid time off, vacation days, and a 401k with a match. In the contracts I've seen, these can vary widely. Some places offer a 401k, but don't match your contribution; others give you only small amounts of vacation. If you work as an independent contractor, you will likely not get benefits.[5] However, your salary should increase to compensate for this.

BILLING

During the hiring process, you might need to sign a document explaining that they won't tell you how much they bill. This is not exclusive to large companies. What this document does is essentially skim off the top and obfuscate numbers. If they can bill $1000 for a complicated critical patient visit and pay you $200, well, you'll never know. Some of it goes to the hospital. Some to administration. Some for pure profit. Some to you. (I'm not saying you should get *everything*, but let's be fair!).

Some companies are sneaky about how they pay you. For example, a colleague went into ER for one of these groups. He gets paid by the relative value unit (RVU). What do they pay for the RVU? Who knows? They don't' say. How many RVUs does he make per patient? Who knows? Salary disagreement? Who cares, you're replaceable. If you won't do the job, some schlub coming out of residency will do it for us. Probably for less money. Good luck to you. We own everything in this area.

If this isn't bad enough, the contract says you're still liable for fraud based on what they bill. Meaning, if they screw up and charge someone a lot of money when it's not indicated, you're on the hook. It does not sound exactly fair, does it?

SUMMARY

All in all, residency is very challenging. Some don't make it (I had three colleagues leave my own program). When considering medicine, consider the entire process of residency. Consider that a significant amount of time will be spent working and the detrimental effects it will have on you, your relationships, and your mental and physical health. It may not be worth it.

- Residency is very challenging, and you will be working 80-100 hours a week.
- Although the ACGME sets rules for resident work hours, these are not followed strictly.
- Depending on your specialty, you may be subject to 24 to 36-hour shifts.
- Companies take advantage of new residents through one sided contracts. They may use geographic restrictions, skimp on malpractice insurance, obfuscate billing, and not pay benefits.

6

CORRUPTION

Unfortunately, physicians are no more immune to corruption than anyone else.

Consider the following scenario. A particular orthopedic residency spot is very competitive. Many qualified candidates apply for the position. The program interviews most of them. Then, one candidate, not so qualified, interviews. The day of the interview, the candidate appears not to care. The other residents do not think this candidate is a good fit. "He won't match," they say. They tell their residency program director their opinions.

The candidate's behavior might seem a little strange to an outside observer. He makes the odd bet to apply to only one program, specifically *this* orthopedic program. The other candidates interviewing apply to many programs. They want to be an orthopedist, and while they may not get their top spot, they know that the more programs they apply to, the better their chances of getting a spot somewhere.

Our candidate disagrees. He is confident he will get in.

Surprisingly, he is right. His bet pays off. He is accepted. Others are stunned.

How did this happen? Why, with money and connections, of course. In medicine, much as in life, the most qualified applicant doesn't always get the job. In this case (the details of this particular story are fictitious), our candidate's father is a prominent academic orthopedist. He recently opened up a new practice with the residency program director. The father poured money into the new practice, and in return his (not so qualified) son got a spot. This happens more than you think. Ask any physician, and they'll tell you a slightly different version of the same story.

PHARMACEUTICAL COMPANIES

We have already discussed the outrageous price hikes pharmaceutical companies engage in. More intelligent people than I have spoken about pharmaceutical companies, pharmacy benefit managers, and their impact on healthcare. As a physician (or hopeful physician), you will be front and center in their impact as you prescribe their products. You will also be exposed to more than your fair share of pharmaceutical representatives.

The amount of pharmaceutical contact you have will vary based on your specialty. But some regular contact is inevitable, as it is the nature of the business. It might happen like this: you will be working and your office manager or boss will tell you there is a pharmaceutical representative who would like to speak to you. You might tell them yes, or if you are working at a hospital, you might stop by where they are, as often they bring food.

For example, imagine Dr. Skin is a well-known dermatologist. She is visited one day by a pharmaceutical representative who wants her to prescribe his company's product. He is always very nice and charming. He offers to take Dr. Skin and her staff to a very expensive restaurant; all expenses will be covered by his employer. He only wants Dr. Skin to promise to consider prescribing his brand-name drug, and the more she does, the more he will be around. Dr. Skin loves the dinners. They take place at her favorite restaurant, where she consistently manages to over-indulge in alcohol use. She finds herself prescribing the drug more and more. She tells her patients it works better. In reality, there are generic versions of the same medicine available, with little to no difference in efficacy. The generic equivalent is much less expensive and less costly to the health care system overall. Nonetheless, she continues to prescribe it, and the pharmaceutical rep continues to schedule more dinners to "discuss" the drug.

Pharmaceutical companies have also been known to throw lavish, ostentatious parties. They invite many physicians, provide unlimited top-tier alcohol and food, and even invite celebrities to harp on just how good a product is. Studies have shown that payments to physicians in the form of food, dinners, parties, etc. to prescribe a drug result in more physicians prescribing the drug [43].

Some cancer doctors even get money from administering certain types of chemotherapy or other medicines, so the problem is widespread [44]. Other physicians were complicit in facilitating the opioid crisis. Always keep in mind that the pharmaceutical company *might* be after money, and that the priorities of your patient should always come first.

SUMMARY

Not all physicians are solely in medicine to treat the sick. They may be in it to enrich themselves, and some might do it in nefarious ways.

- Corruption happens in medicine; the best candidate doesn't always get the job.
- The pharmaceutical industry is more influential than physicians think.
- Some physicians prescribe expensive drugs and receive benefits in return.

7

THE 2020 CORONAVIRUS PANDEMIC

In early 2020, the novel coronavirus (COVID-19) swept through the United States. As of September 2, 2020, there were over 6,004,443 cases in the U.S., with 183,050 deaths [45]. America's healthcare system suddenly had to deal with an overwhelming number of patients. Hospitals in New York City were especially hard hit. A field hospital was set up in Central Park, a naval hospital ship (the USNS Comfort) arrived to assist beleaguered medical workers. One physician described Elmhurst Hospital, an epicenter of the outbreak in New York City, as "apocalyptic" [46]. The failures of the healthcare system were never more apparent. Physicians and other healthcare providers were thrust into the line of fire without much support.

Imagine you are a physician working at the beginning of the pandemic. Suddenly, an influx of patients appears, and many of them are in critical condition. You think to yourself, "The hospital and government will give me the support I need." How wrong you are.

In some states, shelter-in-place orders are delayed. The number of cases increases exponentially. Suddenly, you have many more critical patients than ventilators or ICU beds. A patient comes into the hospital with severe COVID-19 and the need for a ventilator. What do you do? Like other physicians around the country, you are asked to play God [47].

COVID-19 testing sites are nonexistent or sparse. Non-sick patients come to the hospital for tests unnecessarily. It has become so bad that the hospital administration has finally taken notice. They set up a screening site outside the hospital. Even then, the system is not ideal, as some patients die waiting to be seen. Those who survive wait for beds, their oxygen low, their breaths quick and shallow.

You ponder to yourself how such an event can occur in America, one of the richest countries in the world. Yet it does. A truck holding the bodies of those who have died waits outside your hospital, and you have a feeling it will be full before the end of the day [48].

Personal protective equipment (PPE) becomes limited. You have to reuse N95 masks. Sterilizing and re-using the masks could decrease their effectiveness, but what else can you do? There are none left for you [49].

A nurse speaks out against the lack of protective equipment. She states that the safety of her staff is affected. She is fired. This happens around the country [50].

CEO's and hospital administration state that they are losing money; lucrative procedures are canceled. They will be cutting your salary by 50%. Their salary will be unaffected. They continue to rake in millions. You continue to work on the front lines.

Reports soon emerge of your physician colleagues getting sick. Perhaps it is from re-using PPE, but this can never be proven. The physician staff is strained already, and although administration attempts to hire more physicians, you have to deal for the time being. The patient burden increases still more. Later, you learn some of your colleagues have passed away from complications of the virus [51].

You are exhausted after every shift. You have family at home and do not want to infect them. You attempt to stay in a hotel to keep them safe. You have not seen them for weeks, and you are not sure when you will be able to return.

Certain people protest against stay-at-home orders. They claim the virus is a hoax. The government decides to ease social distancing and open up certain business. The amount of daily cases has not gone down yet. You can imagine things will only get worse. Soon, a resurgence of cases occurs. Florida, Texas California, and other states report increasing cases.

It feels like your work and sacrifice are for no reason.

The COVID-19 pandemic has shown that the healthcare system in America is a bloated, inefficient broken mess that shows little care for and gives little support to its employees and patients. Its inability to plan for a catastrophic event is more than telling. When government support was needed most, the response was more than lacking. Physicians, healthcare providers, and staff are essentially managing the whole pandemic by themselves, and things may get worse.

SUMMARY

As of August 2020, the COVID-19 pandemic was still ongoing. Cases continue to increase and there is no end in sight. The COVID-19 pandemic strained an already broken healthcare system.

- Healthcare staff on the frontlines suffered from being overworked and under-supported. Some passed away.
- Administration fired staff who spoke out against

horrid conditions. They collected record compensation while cutting physician and staff salary.
- Physicians and staff fight COVID-19 as much as they fight stupidity. Stupidity is winning.

8

OTHER ISSUES

W hile the following are not large systematic issues that plague physicians, they are certainly worth mentioning. Every physician will be subject to these matters at some point in their career.

VIP PATIENTS

If you're a physician, you'll probably have to deal with "special patients." VIPs, or "very important patients" as they are called, are a miserable pain in your butt. Typically, they will be someone "important" at your hospital, such as the CEO or an executive. It also might just be someone with oodles of money. Usually, the only qualifier for being a "VIP" is that you have more money than the average patient or you are connected to the hospital in some "important" way.

In my experience, these patients can be some of the worst. Not only do they usually come across as entitled, but they frequently take you away from your *real* work (you know, trying to save lives) to ask you to adjust the thermostat. Almost everyone hates dealing with these patients. They complain easily, they expect to be waited on hand and foot, and in my opinion are usually some of the least appreciative. Not every "VIP" is like this, but you might need to prepare for the worst.

It is my opinion that having oodles and oodles of money should not make you a priority in the hospital. In my experience, all you get for dealing with these patients is maybe a nice letter if you do a good job, and a whole lot of trouble if you do one not to their liking. Expect to deal with more of them in your career as a physician. While not a large complaint about the field of medicine, it is an annoyingly real one, nonetheless.

OTHER PHYSICIANS

Finally, as if all the other stuff didn't dissuade you from becoming a physician, you'll have to deal with some of the most difficult people on the planet: other physicians themselves.

If you are an ER or internal medicine physician, good luck. If you want to consult a specialist on a case, it will likely be an uphill battle. Specialists often do not want to see the patient, give excuses, and generally don't want to do their job. You'll have a rock-solid case of bone-sticking-out-of-body and the surgeon might tell you to discharge her.

You'll start to abhor other physicians.

If you are a specialist, such as a surgeon or ENT, good luck. You will get consulted for everything. If you work in dermatology, every rash could be deadly, and the consulting physician tells you how to do your job. It will seem at times that your colleagues have no idea what they are doing. You'll be called to the hospital when the individual could have been seen as an outpatient and feel as if your valuable time is being wasted.

And goodness gracious, the egos of some of the people you work with. They believe they are God's greatest gift to humanity. They will yell, shout, and scream that you are incompetent. The staff will be on edge around them. Professionalism will go out the window. In my training, I had an attending threaten me with violence if I didn't listen. Shouting matches between physicians of different specialties was not as rare as it should have been. I have even seen physicians throw HIV positive blood at others in an heated argument.

You might even be lucky enough to deal with a physician with the words "VIP Physician" on their white coat. What did they do to get this title? Most likely, they did not pass any special tests. Most of the time, they placed that badge there themselves, to establish an aura of their own inflated importance.

Why might it be it this way? Think about it: physicians spend most of their lives reading books and studying. Due to the pressures of medical school, residency, and medicine in general, bedside manner may not be emphasized. Those physicians already deficient become worse throughout the process. Not only does this lack of social graces transfer over to patient care, it also transfers over to interactions with other physicians. This may be why we see the sometimes dysfunctional relationship physicians have amongst themselves today.

SUMMARY

No matter what specialty you go into, you are guaranteed to deal with colleagues who are less than pleasant to talk to. Not a deal-breaker, but it adds unnecessary stress and anguish and shifts focus away from doing what is best for the patient.

- You might have to deal with so-called "VIP Patients," who take up a lot of time. You should ignore them at your own peril.
- Consulting physicians and consultants have a tumultuous relationship.
- Other physicians have massive egos and will scream and call you names in ways you did not think was possible.

9

YOU SHOULD NOT BE A DOCTOR

B eing a physician is great in theory but challenging in practice. You will have to deal with a whole world of nonsense not readily apparent to the outside observer. While the actual practice of clinical medicine is fantastic, the increased amount of time spent on the non-clinical aspects of medicine is less than ideal.

If you are a pre-medical student, consider very carefully if being a physician is right for you. You must pay with time and cash (the average medical school attendee has over $200k in debt), only to be confronted with the reality of medicine [52]. Imagine pouring years of your life into books, taking tests, and accumulating debt only to discover that medicine is more about the bottom line. (Well, lucky for you, you don't need to do that; I have said it a million times in this book). It's easy then to see why maybe you shouldn't be a physician. Why would you, when you can't even do what physicians do? Your position is becoming more and more about money and statistics.

If you are someone curious about the physician life, I

hope to have shed light on the challenges faced by physicians around the country every day.

If, after reading all this, medicine is still appealing to you, then by all means go for it. But if you have any doubts whatsoever, please, please, consider your options and future carefully. Perhaps it would be a good idea to shadow or volunteer at a hospital or clinic. Perhaps you can speak candidly to physicians there and see if they agree with the thoughts and observations in this book. You don't want to be one of the half of all physicians who are dissatisfied with their jobs.

Signed,

A concerned physician.

FOOTNOTES

2. NON-CLINICAL DUTIES

1. They need to be linked to ICD-10 codes, which I won't go over here. Trust me, it's not worth it.
2. I try to finish all my charts at work. But usually, even with all the macros and shortcuts, one or two might slip by and annoy me later.
3. "No! Of course not!" your director might say. "Do what is best for the patient!" Then later he will tell you how you are doing too many CT scans.
4. Of Course, Dr. Good's name has been changed. People like to fire.

3. MALPRACTICE

1. Many physicians choose to fight lawsuits for this reason; however, you risk losing and having an absurd judgment against you.

4. TIME AND MONEY

1. Spoiler: We don't.
2. The cost includes room and board, tuition, fees, and books.
3. As an undergraduate, you may borrow up to $9,500 in your first year; year 2, up to $10,500; and years 3 and beyond, up to $12,500. That might cover your tuition but not much else [53].
4. Technically, Amazon made $5 million in 2001, but it consistently made profit after 2004 [54].
5. You might need 1000-2000 hours of clinical experience before you can practice. 2000 hours is the equivalent of about 16 months.

5. RESIDENCY

1. The Accreditation Council for Graduate Medical Education (ACGME) is the organizational body that oversees resident training programs in the U.S.
2. Being on "house call" means you are at the hospital always ready to answer a question or manage a new patient with a phone you carry around with you. For example, a resident trauma surgeon has finished

seeing all his patients and is sleeping at the hospital overnight. They still get "called" to manage every new trauma patient that comes in, even overnight.

3. Being on "at-home call" means you have finished all your clinical duties and are at home. You may still be called into the hospital to manage a patient or answer a question. It's great.

4. "Rounding" typically includes a brief history and exam. This attending's input would usually be a quick hello and see you later.

5. The difference between an employee and an independent contractor can be a little complicated. Essentially, an employee gets taxes withheld but gets benefits; an independent contractor has no taxes withheld. Usually, independent contractors pay taxes at the end of the year but can also "write off" more, lowering their taxable income. There are pros and cons to each; it is worth researching separately before signing a contract.

APPENDIX: COMMON TERMS AND THEIR DEFINITIONS

ACGME: Accreditation Council for Graduate Medical Education. It certifies residency programs in the USA.

AMA: American Medical Association

At-Home Call: You are at home, but you may still be called into the hospital to manage a patient or called to answer a question.

Attending: a fully-fledged physician who has finished all training.

Boards: An attending physician takes their board exam to become certified in their field.

CME: Continuing Medical Education. CME is learning done by attending physicians to stay current in their field. Every state medical board has CME requirements.

CMS: Centers for Medicaid and Medicare Services

ED: Emergency Department. Also known as Emergency Room (ER).

EMR: Electronic medical record. Used to write notes, put in orders, and discharge patients.

ER: Emergency room. Interchangeable with Emergency Department (ED).

GPA: Grade point average. A 4.00 is usually equivalent to an "A" Average.

House Call: You are at the hospital always ready to answer a question or manage a new patient with a phone you carry around with you, even if it is in the middle of the night.

Inpatient: A patient who is admitted to the hospital.

Intern: A first-year resident physician. They typically just graduated medical school.

MCAT: Medical College Admissions test. A test that is required to get into medical school

Medical student: A non-physician who is studying to be a physician. They usually do clinical rotations with physicians and resident physicians in their 3rd and 4th year of medical school.

NP: Nurse practitioner. A nurse who has completed a higher level of training; they are able to manage and treat patients. In some states they can do this independently, and in others they need the supervision of a physician.

NPDB: National Practitioner Data Bank

Outpatient: A patient who is getting tests outside the hospital (at a clinic)

PA: Physician's assistant. A healthcare provider who is able to manage and treat patients. In some states they can do this independently, and in others they need the supervision of a physician.

PPE: Personal protective equipment

Resident: A training physician who graduated medical school and is training in a specific specialty. After they finish their training, they become an attending.

Rotations: Medical students and residents typically work with physicians in different specialties. When they do this, they are said to be on "rotations." They do this to get exposure to the different fields of medicine.

RVU: Relative value unit. Used to determine physician

reimbursement. The more complicated the patient is to manage, the more RVUs you get.

Specialty: A specific focus of physician training. You can choose, for example, to specialize in internal medicine, anesthesiology, dermatology, or some other field.

USMLE: United States Medical Licensing Examination. Comes in 3 parts (USMLE 1, 2, 3). Medical students and residents take these tests. Equivalent to the COMLEX (which is for osteopathic physicians).

WORKS CITED

[1] M. Leslie Kane, "Medscape National Physician Burnout, Depression & Suicide Report 2019," 16 January 2019. [Online]. Available: https://www.medscape.-com/slideshow/2019-lifestyle-burnout-depression-6011056.

[2] M. Dike Drummond, "Physician Burnout: Its Origin, Symptoms, and Five Main Causes," Sept 2015. [Online]. Available: https://www.aafp.org/fpm/2015/0900/p42.html. [Accessed 2019].

[3] U.S Centers for Medicare & Medicaid Services, "MIPS Overview," 2020. [Online]. Available: https://qpp.cms.-gov/mips/overview.

[4] U.S Centers for Medicare & Medicaid Services, "Quality Measures Requirements," 2020. [Online]. Available: https://qpp.cms.gov/mips/quality-measures?py=2020.

[5] M. F. C. Elizabeth Woodcock, "The MIPS mess Docs Weigh Pulling Out of MIPS Over Paltry Payments," 29 January 2020. [Online]. Available: https://pnh-p.org/news/the-mips-mess/. [Accessed 11 August 2020].

[6] A. Krell, "Doctor denied patients unnecessary opioids.

Their complaints hurt her career, she said," The News Tribune, 07 October 2019. [Online]. Available: https://www.thenewstribune.com/news/local/article235764152.html. [Accessed 16 July 2020].

[7] M. M. Joshua J. Fenton, M. Anthony F. Jerant, M. M. Klea D. Bertakis and e. al, "The Cost of Satisfaction A National Study of Patient Satisfaction, Health Care Utilization, Expenditures, and Mortality," *Archives of Internal Medicine,* vol. 172, no. 5, pp. 405-411, 2012.

[8] K. Falkenberg, "Why Rating Your Doctor Is Bad For Your Health," 21 Janurary 2013. [Online]. Available: https://www.forbes.com/sites/kaifalkenberg/2013/01/02/why-rating-your-doctor-is-bad-for-your-health/#88d038e33c58. [Accessed 2019].

[9] M. J. Louise B Andrew, "Physician Suicide," 21 August 2018. [Online]. Available: https://emedicine.medscape.com/article/806779-overview. [Accessed 2019].

[10] P. Anderson, "Physicians Experience Highest Suicide Rate of Any Profession," 7 May 2018. [Online]. Available: https://www.medscape.com/viewarticle/896257. [Accessed 2019].

[11] E. S. Schernhammer, "Taking Their Own Lives — The High Rate of Physician Suicide," 24 Feburary 2014. [Online]. Available: https://www.researchgate.net/profile/Eva_Schernhammer/publication/7784092_Taking_Their_Own_Lives_-_The_High_Rate_of_Physician_Suicide/links/0a85e530b-d7ee22555000000/Taking-Their-Own-Lives-The-High-Rate-of-Physician-Suicide.pdf. [Accessed 2019].

[12] ABC7 Eyewitness News Team Coverage, "Mercy Hospital Shooting: 4 dead, including Chicago Officer Samuel Jimenez and gunman," 19 November 2018. [Online]. Available: https://abc7chicago.com/mercy-hospital-chicago--

medical-center-shooting-active-shooter/4720765/. [Accessed 2 August 2020].

[13] New York Times, Ali Watkins, Michael Rothfeld, William K. Rashbaum and Brian M. Rosenthal, "Top E.R. Doctor Who Treated Virus Patients Dies by Suicide," 27 April 2020. [Online]. Available: https://www.nytimes.com/2020/04/27/nyregion/new-york-city-doctor-suicide-coronavirus.html. [Accessed 02 August 2020].

[14] M. NIRAN AL-AGBA, "Are Health Insurers Practicing Medicine Without A License?," 30 January 2019. [Online]. Available: https://thedeductible.com/2019/01/30/are-health-insurers-practicing-medicine-without-a-license/#more-83. [Accessed 2019].

[15] UnitedHealth Group, "Form 10-Q," 2019. [Online]. Available: https://www.unitedhealthgroup.com/content/dam/UHG/PDF/investors/2019/UNH-Q1-2019-Form-10-Q.pdf.

[16] M. M. Sally Tan, B. Kira Seiger and M. M. e. a. Peter Renehan, "Trends in Private Equity Acquisition of Dermatology Practices in the United States," 2019. [Online]. Available: https://jamanetwork.com/journals/jamadermatology/article-abstract/2738309. [Accessed 2019].

[17] K. Hafner, "Why Private Equity Is Furious Over a Paper in a Dermatology Journal," 26 October 2018. [Online]. Available: https://www.nytimes.com/2018/10/26/health/private-equity-dermatology.html. [Accessed 2019].

[18] Department of Justice Office of Public Affairs, "Two Physician Groups Pay Over $33 Million to Resolve Claims Involving HMA Hospitals," 19 December 2017. [Online]. Available: https://www.justice.gov/opa/pr/two-physician-groups-pay-over-33-million-resolve-claims-involving-hma-hospitals. [Accessed 2019].

[19] NIHCM Foundation, "Hospital Consolidation: Trends, Impacts & Outlook," 2020. [Online]. Available: https://www.nihcm.org/categories/hospital-consolidation-trends-impacts-outlook. [Accessed 2020].

[20] New York Times, Jessica Silver-Greenberg, Jesse Drucker and David Enrich, "Hospitals Got Bailouts and Furloughed Thousands While Paying C.E.O.s Millions," 8 June 2020. [Online]. Available: https://www.nytimes.com/2020/06/08/business/hospitals-bailouts-ceo-pay.html. [Accessed 02 August 2020].

[21] HCA Healthcare Inc, "HCA Healthcare Reports Second Quarter 2020 Results," 22 July 2020. [Online]. Available: https://investor.hcahealthcare.com/news/news-details/2020/HCA-Healthcare-Reports-Second-Quarter-2020-Results/default.aspx. [Accessed 2 August 2020].

[22] K. Thomas, "Patients Eagerly Awaited a Generic Drug. Then They Saw the Price.," 23 Feburary 2018. [Online]. Available: https://www.nytimes.com/2018/02/23/health/valeant-drug-price-syprine.html. [Accessed 2019].

[23] CBS Balitmore, "Cost Jumps Nearly 500-Percent For Life-Saving EpiPens," 18 August 2018. [Online]. Available: https://baltimore.cbslocal.com/2016/08/18/cost-jumps-nearly-500-percent-for-life-saving-epipens/. [Accessed 2019].

[24] K. Thomas, "Express Scripts Offers Diabetes Patients a $25 Cap for Monthly Insulin," 3 April 2019. [Online]. Available: https://www.nytimes.com/2019/04/03/health/drug-prices-insulin-express-scripts.html. [Accessed 2019].

[25] J. L. L. J. A.-B. C. C. a. W. H. S. Niteesh K. Choudhry, "Drug Company–Sponsored Patient Assistance Programs: A Viable Safety Net?," 19 May 2010. [Online]. Available: https://www.ncbi.nlm.nih.gov/pmc/articles/PMC2873618/. [Accessed 2020].

[26] B. S. S. B. M. Hilary Daniel, "Policy Recommenda-tions for Pharmacy Benefit Managers to Stem the Escalating Costs of Prescription Drugs: A Position Paper From the American College of Physicians," 3 December 2019. [Online]. Available: https://www.acpjournals.org/doi/10.7326/M19-0035. [Accessed 16 July 2020].

[27] NEW YORK DAILY NEWS, "Bronx woman awarded more than $110 million in malpractice lawsuit against St. Barnabas Hospital, doctors," 13 April 2019. [Online]. Avail-able: https://www.nydailynews.com/new-york/ny-malprac-tice-barnabas-doctors-bronx-20190413-w6jkcprhszh4jimcwwqgwekqde-story.html. [Accessed 2019].

[28] WAMU, "Largest Medical Malpractice Verdict In U.S. History' Awarded To Maryland Woman," 26 September 2019. [Online]. Available: https://wamu.org/sto-ry/19/09/26/largest-medical-malpractice-verdict-in-u-s-history-awarded-to-maryland-woman/.

[29] C. Broward, "Clay deputy awarded $178 million in lawsuit against Memorial Hospital," 23 January 2012. [Online]. Available: https://www.jacksonville.-com/news/crime/2012-01-23/story/clay-deputy-awarded-178-million-lawsuit-against-memorial-hospital. [Accessed 2019].

[30] AMA, "Medical liability market research," 25 October 2019. [Online]. Available: https://www.ama-assn.org/prac-tice-management/sustainability/medical-liability-market-research. [Accessed 02 August 2020].

[31] Cornell Law School, "Judicial Immunity from Suit," [Online]. Available: https://www.law.cornell.edu/constitu-tion-conan/article-3/section-1/judicial-immunity-from-suit.

[32] Association of American Medical Colleges, ": MCAT and GPA Grid for Applicants and Acceptees to U.S. Medical Schools, 2017-2018 through 2019-2020 (aggregated)," 02

April 2019. [Online]. Available: https://www.aamc.org/system/files/2020-04/2019_FACTS_Table_A-23_0.pdf. [Accessed 01 August 2020].

[33] Educationdata.org, "Average Cost of College & Tuition," 2020. [Online]. Available: https://educationdata.org/average-cost-of-college/. [Accessed 2020].

[34] Federal Student Aid, "Federal Student Loans Programs," [Online]. Available: https://studentaid.gov/sites/default/files/federal-loan-programs.pdf. [Accessed 2020].

[35] M. Leslie Kane, "Medscape Physician Compensation Report 2019," 10 April 2019. [Online]. Available: https://www.medscape.com/slideshow/2019-compensation-overview-6011286#3. [Accessed 2020].

[36] A. M. Martinho, "Becoming a Doctor in Europe: Objective Selection Systems," AMA Journal of Ethics, 2012. [Online]. Available: https://journalofethics.ama-assn.org/article/becoming-doctor-europe-objective-selection-systems/2012-12.

[37] C. J. M. J. A. L. D. B. E. Ajay Tandon, "MEASURING OVERALL HEALTH SYSTEM PERFORMANCE FOR 191 COUNTRIES," 2000. [Online]. Available: https://www.who.int/healthinfo/paper30.pdf. [Accessed 2020].

[38] Association of American Medical Colleges, "Statement by the Association of American Medical Colleges on FY 2017 Appropriations for the Department of Health and Human Services," 15 April 2016. [Online]. Available: https://www.aamc.org/system/files/c/1/458706-aamcfy17s-tatementtohouselabor-hhs-edappropriationssubcommittee.pdf. [Accessed 2020].

[39] José R. Guardado, PhD; AMA, "Policy Research Perspectives," 2018. [Online]. Available: https://www.ama-assn.org/sites/ama-assn.org/files/corp/media-browser/pub-

lic/government/advocacy/policy-research-perspective-liability-insurance-premiums.pdf. [Accessed 2020].

[40] AAMC, "New Findings Confirm Predictions on Physician Shortage," 23 April 2019. [Online]. Available: https://www.aamc.org/news-insights/press-releases/new-findings-confirm-predictions-physician-shortage. [Accessed 2020].

[41] H. a. H. S. Committee, H. Q. Subcommittee, Pigman, (.-I. Bush, Daniels, Jacquet, Magar, Roth, Sabatini, Slosberg and D. Smith, "CS/CS/HB 607: Direct Care Workers," 2020. [Online]. Available: https://www.flsenate.gov/Session/Bill/2020/607 . [Accessed 2020].

[42] ACGME, "ACGME Common Program Requirements (Residency)," 3 February 2020. [Online]. Available: https://www.acgme.org/Portals/0/PFAssets/ProgramRequirements/CPRResidency2020.pdf.

[43] c. s. S. A. d. a. M. K. p. A. K. V. a. p. H. M. K. p. D. M. p. D. B. d. d. J. S. William Fleischman, "Research Association between payments from manufacturers of pharmaceuticals to physicians and regional prescribing: cross sectional ecological study," 16 August 2016. [Online]. Available: https://www.bmj.com/content/354/bmj.i4189. [Accessed 18 July 2020].

[44] Journal of Clinical Oncology, Jennifer L. Malin , Jane C. Weeks , Arnold L. Potosky , Mark C. Hornbrook , Nancy L. Keating, "Medical Oncologists' Perceptions of Financial Incentives in Cancer Care," 2013. [Online]. Available: https://ascopubs.org/doi/full/10.1200/JCO.2012.43.6063. [Accessed 19 July 2020].

[45] CDC, "Cases in the U.S.," 16 July 2020. [Online]. Available: https://www.cdc.gov/coronavirus/2019-ncov/cases-updates/cases-in-us.html. [Accessed 16 July 2020].

[46] S. S. J. G. a. B. M. R. Michael Rothfeld, "13 Deaths in

a Day: An 'Apocalyptic' Coronavirus Surge at an N.Y.C. Hospital," New York Times, 25 March 2020. [Online]. Available: https://www.nytimes.com/2020/03/25/nyregion/nyc-coronavirus-hospitals.html.

[47] J. Sopel, "Coronavirus: The young doctors being asked to play god," BBC, 2 April 2020. [Online]. Available: https://www.bbc.com/news/world-us-canada-52137160.

[48] M. M. a. R. S. C. Brynn Gingras, "For the first time since 9/11, NYC has set up makeshift morgues. This time, it's in anticipation of coronavirus deaths," 26 March 2020. [Online]. Available: https://www.cnn.com/2020/03/26/us/makeshift-morgues-coronavirus-new-york/index.html. [Accessed 2020].

[49] 60 Minutes; Bill Whitaker, "Sick doctors, nurses and not enough equipment: NYC health care workers on the fight against the coronavirus," 12 April 2020. [Online]. Available: https://www.cbsnews.com/news/personal-protective-equipment-ppe-doctors-nurses-short-supply-60-minutes-2020-04-12/.

[50] A. P. P. Michael L. Diamond, "Coronavirus in NJ: Jersey Shore hospital nurse fired as dispute over protective equipment flares," 7 April 2020. [Online]. Available: https://www.app.com/story/news/health/2020/04/07/coronavirus-nj-jersey-shore-hospital-nurse-fired-dispute-protective-equipment/2963609001/. [Accessed 2020].

[51] N. Soo Kim, "MORE THAN 200 DOCTORS AND NURSES HAVE DIED COMBATING CORONAVIRUS ACROSS THE GLOBE," 10 April 2020. [Online]. Available: https://www.newsweek.com/more-200-doctors-nurses-died-combating-coronavirus-1497181. [Accessed 2020].

[52] AAMC, "Medical Student Education: Debt, Costs, and Loan Repayment Fact Card," October 2018. [Online]. Available: https://store.aamc.org/downloadable/download/sample/sample_id/240/.

[53] Department of Education, "Subsidized and Unsubsidized Loans," 2020. [Online]. Available: https://studentaid.gov/understand-aid/types/loans/subsidized-unsubsidized. [Accessed May 2020].

[54] J. Karaian, "Amazon's quarterly net profit," 2018. [Online]. Available: https://theatlas.com/charts/BJjuqbWLz.

[55] New York State Department of Health, "New York State Department of Health COVID-19 Tracker," 2020. [Online]. Available: https://covid19tracker.health.ny.gov/views/NYS-COVID19-Tracker/NYSDOHCOVID-19Tracker-Map?%3Aembed=yes&%3Atoolbar=no&%3Atabs=n. [Accessed 5 May 2020].

ACKNOWLEDGMENTS

Thank you to my girlfriend. Without her, I would have never published this book. Too many hours of hers have been spent editing this book instead of studying. For that, I am eternally and always grateful.

Thanks to my family who supported me in writing this book. Their support in getting my thoughts out was essential. Thank you, mom and dad. To my brothers, try harder (kidding).

Thank you to those friends who helped me launch this book. I felt like I was asking a lot, yet you supported me in my endeavors. I appreciate that more than you can know. It is easier to put this book in the world because of you. Thank you.

Thank you to all the physicians who heard of my book and allowed me to share their stories. I appreciate it.

ABOUT THE AUTHOR

Dr. Patrick Eric Nassir was born and raised in Florida. Interested in medicine and helping others after volunteering in a hospital's busy ER, he began the long journey of becoming a physician. He obtained a medical degree from a school in Florida. After medical school, he began his emergency medicine residency in one of New York City's strained safety net hospitals. His residency was grueling and difficult, as he worked with limited resources and ancillary staff in an area rife with gang violence and the underserved. It was there he first noted the failures of America's healthcare system; it took advantage of patients and healthcare staff.

After graduating, he practiced in a hospital in Florida whose patients ranged from the underserved to the rich. He joined a large physician company (owned by private equity investors). He still practices there to this day, though he has reduced his hours.

After joining, he noted just how little the company seemed to care for the patient and the physician. It seemed to him the company and the healthcare system wanted to use their power in an attempt to make more and more money for the shareholder and the executive, even in "non-profit" hospitals. As time went on, he was more and more inundated with regulations, administrative tasks, and non-clinical duties which stressed him immensely. It seemed to him that medicine was less about helping people and more about numbers, statistics and money. His old residency colleagues spoke to him and shared similar experiences.

He began to think about the entire for-profit healthcare system, its failures, the legal system, the long journey to be a physician, and the changing role of physicians and staff. The tipping point came with America's catastrophic failure in handling the COVID-19 pandemic. Personal protective equipment was lacking, the pandemic was mismanaged by the government, and pay was reduced while executives continued to collect. It was too much.

He then collected his and others' thoughts on what it feels like to be a practicing physician in this country and published *Why You Should Not be a Doctor*.

twitter.com/WhyYouShouldNo1
instagram.com/whyyoushouldnotbeadoctor